21st
Century
Skills Library

COOL CAREERS

COMMERCIAL FISHER

BARBARA A. SOMERVILL

Published in the United States of America by
Cherry Lake Publishing, Ann Arbor, Michigan
www.cherrylakepublishing.com

Content Adviser
Margaret Curole, Commercial Fishermen of America Board Member

Credits
Photos: Cover, pages 1 and 7, ©Alaska Stock LLC/Alamy; pages 4, 10, 15, and 23,
©Photolibrary; page 9, ©Barbara Reddoch/Dreamstime.com; pages 13, 17, and 18,
©Sebastian Czapnik/Dreamstime.com; page 20, ©Jirka13/Dreamstime.com;
page 24, ©Peter Leahy/Dreamstime.com; page 27, ©iStockphoto.com/Aquilegia

Library of Congress Cataloging-in-Publication Data
Somervill, Barbara A.
  Commercial fisher/by Barbara A. Somervill.
    p. cm.—(Cool careers)
  Includes bibliographical references and index.
  ISBN-13: 978-1-60279-986-8 (lib. bdg.)
  ISBN-10: 1-60279-986-5 (lib. bdg.)
  1. Fishers—Juvenile literature. 2. Fish trade—Juvenile literature.
3. Fisheries—Juvenile literature. I. Title.
  HD8039.F65S66 2011
  639.2023—dc22   2010029123

Cherry Lake Publishing would like to acknowledge
the work of The Partnership for 21st Century Skills.
Please visit *www.21stcenturyskills.org* for more information.

Printed in the United States of America
Corporate Graphics Inc.
January 2011
CLSP08

TABLE OF CONTENTS

COMMERCIAL FISHER

CHAPTER ONE
A DAY AT WORK

The *Lexi II* pulls out of an Alaskan harbor in mid-February. It is headed out to the Bering Sea for several weeks of fishing for crabs, or crabbing. This **commercial** fishing vessel is built to survive big 40-foot (12-meter) waves. It's a good thing, because the ship will meet some of these waves during its trip.

Fishers unload a crab pot pulled from the Bering Sea.

The **galley's** freezer and pantry are loaded with meat, cereal, and canned goods. **Deckhands** eat huge meals when they are out at sea. They work 18- to 20-hour shifts. The meals help them keep up their strength.

The *Lexi II* heads toward an area where crabs are often found. Deckhands bait the bulky crab pots that will capture the crabs. Then they throw the pots into the water. A **buoy** marks the location of each crab pot. After the last pot is dropped, the ship returns to haul up the first pots. It may be a day or longer before a pot is brought back on deck. Hopefully, the pot will be full of crabs. Fishers measure and sort the crabs. Crabs that are too small are returned to the sea.

■ ■ ■

Off the coast of Maine, another boatload of commercial fishers heads out to sea. They are in a 113-foot (34-meter) vessel called the *Sunshine.* They will fish for herring. To do this, the crew uses a purse **seine**. This kind of net forms into a pouch, trapping fish inside. Netting fish is hard work. It takes about 2 hours to set up the net and haul it back in. The *Sunshine's* crew works all night to put the net out four or five times.

Many things can go wrong on a fishing trip. Bad weather limits the amount of fish caught. Nets tear, machines break, and people get hurt. **Sonar** can help find fish, but it only works if the fish are nearby. These can all reduce a fishing trip's success.

21ST CENTURY CONTENT

Commercial fishers use different methods for catching different types of fish. In the United States, the two most popular methods are **trawling** and purse seining. Trawling is used to scoop fish and shellfish off the ocean floor. Purse seining is used to catch sardines, tuna, and other **schooling** fish.

Commercial fishers on Canadian waters use similar methods. Gillnetters, seiners, and trollers, for example, are commonly used to harvest salmon.

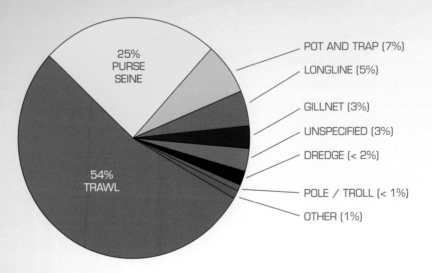

- 25% PURSE SEINE
- 54% TRAWL
- POT AND TRAP (7%)
- LONGLINE (5%)
- GILLNET (3%)
- UNSPECIFIED (3%)
- DREDGE (< 2%)
- POLE / TROLL (< 1%)
- OTHER (1%)

(Source: National Marine Fisheries Service, 2009)

It is important for fishers to take care of their nets and other equipment.

J. C. Darda pulls into the dock. He's back in port because of a hurricane warning. He is one of nearly 15,000 commercial fishers in Louisiana. The state is home to a $2.8 billion fishing industry. Not long ago, a massive oil spill occurred in the Gulf of Mexico. At first, Darda continued to catch as many shrimp as possible before the oil spill polluted local waters. Then the spill spread. Commercial fisheries in Louisiana were in trouble.

An oil spill can kill fish and other animals that live in and around water. Sea animals that do not die may still have poison from the oil in their bodies. A fishery cannot sell seafood that might make people sick. The oil spill brought a big change for Darda and hundreds of other captains. The oil company responsible for the oil spill hired commercial fishing vessels to help control the oil. "I've been fishing 50 years, and this is the first time I ever had a boss," says Darda. "Still, I'm out on the water. That's my life."

■ ■ ■

After most of the oil was cleaned from the water's surface and beaches, government agencies tested the fish and shellfish in the Gulf to make sure it was safe to eat. Darda and the rest of Louisiana's commercial fishers went back to doing what they love. "When I'm on the water, that's where I belong," Darda says. "For me, my job is not work. I trawl because I love it."

The 2010 Gulf Coast oil spill has been called the worst spill in U.S. history.

CHAPTER TWO
LEARNING THE SKILLS

Commercial fishing is often a family business. Many of today's fishers learned their trade from their parents.

Commercial fishers share a love for life on the water.

That was the case for J. C. Darda, whose father, grandfather, and great-grandfather were fishermen before him. "I was out on the ships when I was seven," he says. "I ran a boat with a deckhand when I was twelve." In this way, love of the water is passed down from one generation to the next.

Some fishers begin as greenhorns, or people who have never worked at sea before. But that is rare. Fred Dockery got into commercial fishing as a greenhorn. He now runs his own boat out of Charleston. "I was going to be a writer," he says. "I was living in New England. I had no money and no food. A friend offered me his slot on a commercial fishing vessel, and I took it. I was hooked from day one." Dockery's first experience was a rough way to start, with freezing weather and long hours. But commercial fishing changed his life. "It's emotional more than anything else," Dockery explains. "When I see other ships going out and I can't go, I literally get sick to my stomach. I love the water, the wide-open spaces, and the sense of freedom."

There are no education requirements for being a commercial fisher, but there are ways to improve your chances of getting hired. It is helpful to take courses in **navigation**, boat handling, and boat safety. Knowing how to repair machinery and radios is also a plus. First-aid skills are useful when accidents happen. Fishers can learn these skills by taking classes at vocational schools and community colleges.

LIFE & CAREER SKILLS

Safety is a priority on commercial fishing vessels. The Coast Guard offers classes for fishers to learn the safety skills they need. A crew should be trained in fighting fires, cardiopulmonary resuscitation (CPR), and first aid. When a crew passes these classes, they receive a safety certificate for their boat.

You might be surprised that cooking is an important skill for commercial fishers. Fishing crews need to eat, and the better the food, the happier the crew. A cooking course at a community college or vocational school is a good investment. Many deckhands work both on deck and in the galley.

It might seem like being captain would be the best job on a commercial fishing vessel, but being captain is not easy. The captain works hard and is responsible for both the **catch** and the crew. Some captains own their vessels. Others are hired by owners to run ships. It is the captain's job to plan and oversee the fishing operation. This means finding the best fishing spots, making sure equipment is in good shape, managing the catch, and selling the fish.

Deckhands work to clean the catch.

LEARNING & INNOVATION SKILLS

Networking can help you land a job on a commercial fishing boat. Visit commercial fishing trade shows and waterfront events. Talk to people about what they do. Be friendly and collect business cards so you can keep in touch. You can also meet new people at public meetings where commercial fishing issues are discussed. Unless you are a member of a fishing family, it is hard to break into commercial fishing. Building a network will make it easier.

Captains must be able to use a compass, read charts, and use electronic navigation equipment such as GPS systems. They also need to know how to use sonar. Sonar can track schools of fish and help the captain avoid underwater obstacles such as sandbars and reefs.

Captains also need to be leaders. They need to hire good crews that get along well in tough conditions. During emergencies, captains depend on their crews to work together and overcome problems.

Captains and **first mates** on vessels that weigh 200 tons or more need licenses. Licenses are also required

Fishing boat crews must work as a team.

for some jobs on vessels on which fish are caught, cleaned, and prepared for sale. The Coast Guard issues these licenses, which can be renewed online.

Not everyone is suited to work on a commercial fishing vessel, but there are many other jobs in related fields. Shipbuilders create new vessels and technology to help crews catch more fish. Maintenance crews keep the old vessels running smoothly. Workers are also needed to make and sell the nets, **winches**, crab pots, and other equipment used by fishers.

21ST CENTURY CONTENT

Commercial fishing has gone high-tech. Fishing captains now sell their catches over the Internet. They post their catches online. Restaurants, fish shops, and grocery stores look through the catches and place their orders. The catch is often sold by the time the fishing vessel docks.

Conservationists work with the fishing industry to protect the environment. Some work as observers on fishing vessels. Others work in fishery management or for conservation groups. Environmentalists make sure that food fish species survive. They also make sure fishing does not have a bad effect on our environment.

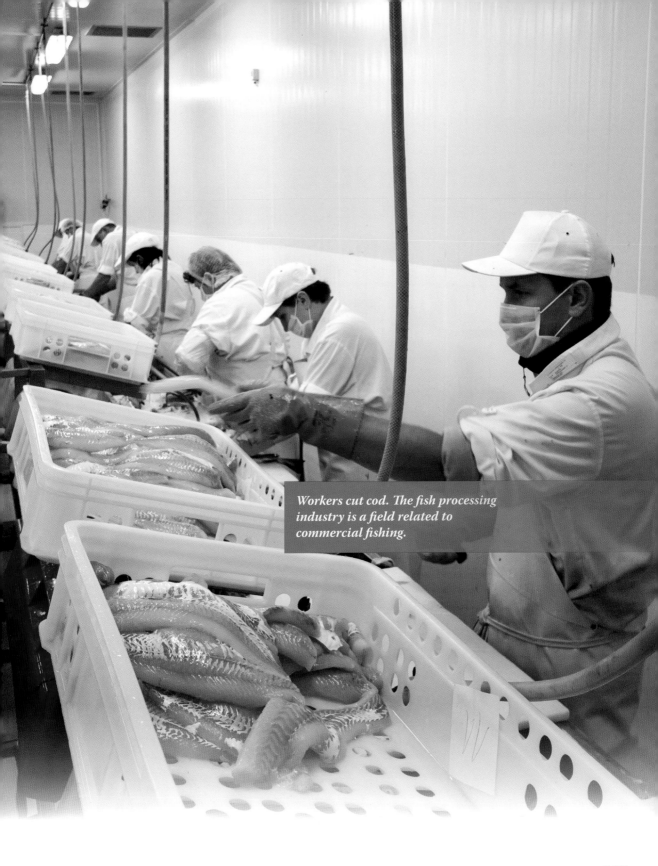

Workers cut cod. The fish processing industry is a field related to commercial fishing.

CHAPTER THREE
DEMANDS OF THE JOB

Commercial fishing is demanding work. Hauling in fish or shellfish requires a strong, healthy body.

Fishers often wear hats and coats to stay warm in wet and chilly weather.

Deckhands also deal with foul weather and the chance of injuries. Crab fishing in Alaska takes place in winter, when the seas and weather are at their worst.

LEARNING & INNOVATION SKILLS

Commercial fishers used to have trouble getting catches to the market quickly. Some companies that sell frozen fish do not worry about that problem anymore. They have huge processing vessels that can catch, clean, and package fish on the ship. When a processing vessel pulls into the harbor, it unloads packaged, frozen fish that is ready for sale in a supermarket.

Commercial fishing is one of the most dangerous jobs in the world. Bad storms and high seas can sink boats. The Coast Guard tries to keep fishing vessels safe, but there is no guarantee. Fires also happen on boats. A fire at sea can destroy a vessel and cost lives.

Fifty commercial fishers were killed on the job in 2008. This gave commercial fishing the highest death rate of all jobs in the United States. A commercial fisher in the United States is 30 times more likely to die in a work-related situation than in any other industry. Commercial fishing has similar death rates in other countries.

Most serious fishing accidents happen when crews are spreading or pulling in fishing gear. Deckhands have gotten caught in nets and suffered broken bones or deep cuts.

Fishers may suffer from back pain from bending and lifting on the job.

LEARNING & INNOVATION SKILLS

NIOSH is the National Institute for Occupational Safety and Health. NIOSH researchers find ways to reduce accidents on the job. Researchers found that serious accidents happened when deckhands got tangled in nets when a winch was moving. They designed and tested an emergency stop switch that would stop the deck winch if someone got caught in the nets. The system was tested on vessels during the 2005–2007 fishing seasons. It was able to prevent accidents and is now widely used.

An experienced commercial fisher may earn about $44,000 per year. Beginners should not expect to earn as much. Most deckhands are paid by the day or by a percentage of the profit. A worker signs on for a trip. Trips can last anywhere from a few days to several months. Pay is offered based on the worker's experience and the length and difficulty of the job. A day fee might be as much as $700 for some jobs.

Pay for commercial fishing work sometimes depends on two factors. The first is how much it costs to run the vessel. The second is how many fish the vessel catches. One crew might spend a week at sea and catch as many fish as they are legally allowed to take. Another crew could spend the same amount of time and catch very little.

The cost of running a fishing vessel can affect how much money commercial fishers earn. Fishing vessels are expensive in Alaska, where fishing is a big business. A new salmon vessel might cost about $325,000. Then there is the cost of nets, permits, fuel, food, and safety equipment. Captains may also need permits to fish in certain areas. Fishery permits can cost thousands of dollars.

Some crews are paid by a percentage of the ship's profit. The captain and owner get the most money. The rest is divided among the crew. A deckhand might make as much as 15 to 20 percent of the total profit.

Fishers don't know what the day will bring. They might have a great catch one day, and a bad catch on the next.

CHAPTER FOUR
A FUTURE IN COMMERCIAL FISHING

Commercial fishing was once a huge opportunity. There were few rules or laws. Fishers got rich whaling, catching salmon, or pulling in tuna. That is no longer the case.

In 2010, New York State set a quota for the number of black sea bass that could be caught.

It is much harder to make a profit in today's commercial fishing industry.

The law requires fishing vessels and their captains to have licenses or permits. Each state sets its own rules for licenses. These rules can get complicated. Fred Dockery owns three boats and works all year. He crabs throughout the year, shrimps in the summer, and farms clams. "In South Carolina," he says, "I buy a commercial fishing license for $25. For shrimping, my boat needs a license. For crabbing, you buy your license by how many crab pots you have. The average is about 100–150 pots."

Other states' laws are different than South Carolina's. Most only give out a certain number of licenses. A new fisher cannot just buy a new license and go fishing. He must buy an existing license from someone who is willing to sell theirs. Because most fishers love being at sea, there are few licenses for sale.

Fishing seasons and species quotas are newer ideas. In the past, fishing crews would catch as many fish or shellfish as their vessels could hold. No one thought that the oceans might run out of Atlantic cod or flounder.

However, certain areas and species were overfished. Today, states set quotas on different fish species. A quota may limit the amount of fish a crew can catch in a certain time period. It might also place a limit on what size the fish can be. For example, fishers might only be allowed to keep fish that are more than 18 inches (45.7 centimeters) long.

Experts keep track of how many fish are caught. The quotas are adjusted to make sure all fish species will continue to survive. Chilean sea bass, Atlantic salmon, swordfish, and dozens of other species have all had quotas.

The commercial fishing industry is not limited to just catching fish. Some people are in charge of making sure there will be enough fish for people to eat in the future. Many commercial fisheries now hire marine conservation biologists. These scientists study crab populations in the Bering Sea, oyster beds in a bay, and many other sources of sea life. They figure out ways to fix any problems they find. One place where conservation is helping to fix major problems is Chesapeake Bay.

21ST CENTURY CONTENT

Conservation groups keep a close eye on problems caused by **bycatch**. When tuna fishers accidentally catch dolphins, the dolphins are by-catch. Another example of by-catch is when sea turtles get tangled up in nets. Sea birds such as the albatross can be caught in **longlines** and drowned. Conservationists worry when endangered species get caught in commercial fishing nets. Commercial fishers have developed ways to reduce by-catch. For example, they now put turtle excluders in nets. These devices keep sea turtles from getting caught.

This fish is caught in a shrimp net. Scientists, net makers, and fishers must work together to reduce bycatch.

For many years, people harvested oysters from the floor of the Chesapeake Bay. About one hundred years ago, the bay was producing 10 million bushels of oysters each year. Disease, pollution, loss of habitat, and overfishing turned the bay into a dead zone. Today, a massive oyster recovery program is working to return the Chesapeake Bay to health. When oyster beds recover, well-managed commercial fishing will keep the problem from happening again.

21ˢᵀ CENTURY CONTENT

According to the United Nations Environment Program, scientists have identified nearly 150 dead zones in the world's oceans. A dead zone is a place where pollution has affected the sea. In a dead zone, there is not enough oxygen in the water to support life. Fish move out of dead zones quickly. Clams, lobsters, and oysters move more slowly. Many of them die. Fishing is not allowed in dead zones. There are well-known dead zones in the Gulf of Mexico and the Chesapeake Bay.

Increased costs and decreased amounts of fish make it harder for commercial fishers to profit. New rules, conservation issues, and higher fuel prices can also make things difficult. However, the worldwide demand for seafood continues to rise. "There will always be fishing," says Fred Dockery. "People love seafood. Commercial fishing won't be like what it looks like today. It will change." For fishers like Dockery, Darda, and thousands of others, commercial fishing isn't a career. It's a way of life.

WELL-KNOWN FISHERS AND FISHING ORGANIZATIONS

Phil Harris (1956–2010) was a commercial fishing captain who was best known as the subject of the TV show *Deadliest Catch*. He worked in the fishing industry for more than 30 years. He spent 18 of those years as captain and co-owner of the *Cornelia Marie*, a successful crabbing vessel.

Commercial Fishermen of America is an organization that promotes the commercial fishing industry. They help fishers network and find new jobs. They also help educate people about commercial fishing and protecting the environment.

Fisheries Council of Canada is a group of about 100 Canadian fishing companies that work together to protect Canada's commercial fishing industry.

United Fishermen of Alaska is made up of 37 fishing organizations that work together to promote the commercial fishing industry in Alaska. They work to make sure laws are fair to fishers. They also educate people about environmental and safety issues.

GLOSSARY

buoy (BOO-ee) floating marker

bycatch (BYE-kach) unwanted animals that are trapped when fishing

catch (KACH) the total number of fish caught on a fishing trip

commercial (kuh-MUR-shuhl) having to do with business

deckhands (DEK-handz) sailors who perform work that requires strength and a lot of energy

first mates (FURST MAYTS) officers just below the rank of captain on commercial ships

galley (GA-lee) a kitchen on a ship, plane, or camper

longlines (LONG-lynz) long fishing lines with many baited hooks attached

navigation (na-vuh-GAY-shuhn) plotting the route of a ship or aircraft

networking (NET-wurk-ing) meeting new people who can help you get jobs

schooling (SKOO-ling) traveling together in groups called schools

seine (SAYN) a type of fishing net that closes up like a pouch

sonar (SOH-nahr) a method for detecting objects in water using sound waves

trawling (TRAW-ling) fishing with a net along the seafloor

winches (WIN-chez) tools used for hauling or pulling

FOR MORE INFORMATION

BOOKS

Beech, Linda. *The Exxon Valdez Deadly Oil Spill*. New York: Bearport Publishing Company, 2007.

Lourie, Peter. *Whaling Season: A Year in the Life of an Arctic Whale Scientist*. Boston: Houghton Mifflin Books, 2009.

WEB SITES

Commercial Fishermen of America
www.cfafish.org
Find out more about this organization that supports commercial fishers in the United States.

The Ocean Conservancy
www.oceanconservancy.org
Discover ways that you can help preserve our oceans and seas and the species that live there.

Voices from the Fisheries
www.st.nmfs.noaa.gov/voicesfromthefisheries
Hear what fishers have to say about their work and their lives.

INDEX

ABOUT THE AUTHOR

Compared to commercial fishing, Barbara Somervill thinks her job is easy. She has been writing books for children for more than a dozen years. Most of her work deals with science, social studies, and biographies. Her writing gives her an opportunity to learn new things all the time, which is why she loves it. She says, "This book gave me a close look into a really difficult career. I truly appreciate people who fish because I love salmon and seafood."